Sing!

Memorize!

Acts 2:1-4

Holy Spirit!

To Christy, Zach, Mariama, Lydia, Olivia, Acacia, Daso, and Blessing,

You are the most Spirit-filled friend (and family) I can think of! Thank you for being my roommate in college when no one else wanted me. Thank you for serving Jesus in Nigeria. Thank you for loving Him so passionately that it resounds in all that you do. Thank you for loving God's Word enough to work with Wycliffe and translate it into other languages. Everyone deserves to have God's Word in their own language! You helped grow my faith and love for the Lord, and I treasure that in you.

Your Roomie in Spirit,
Amie

No part of this publication may be reproduced by any means without written permission of the author, but she's pretty nice and is likely to say yes. You might as well give it a try.

ISBN: 9798307763391

Imprint: Independently published by Amie Winningham
Copyright 2025

Music written by Amie Winningham
Music sung by Taylor Cobos
Photographs by Amie Winningham

singmoveandmemorize.com
Other books in series available on Amazon.com
Corresponding video lessons and curriculum at teacherspayteachers.com

Music

Scan the QR code to listen to the music and start memorizing God's Word!

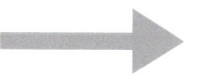 

When the <u>day</u> of Pentecost came,

Hand comes down to meet flat arm.

they were all together in one place.

Point out and around.

Suddenly

Snap then two thumbs up.

a sound like
the blowing
of a violent
<u>wind</u>

Two jazz hands wave side to side.

came
from heaven

Circle hands above head.

and filled the whole <u>house</u> where they were siting.

Fingertips touch to make a house.

They saw what seemed to be tongues of <u>fire</u>

Dance two jazz hands up and down.

that separated and came to rest on each of them.

Touch the back of both hands.

All of <u>them</u>

Point out and around.

were filled with the Holy Spirit

Two okay signs pull a string apart.

and began to speak in other tongues

Touch fingertips to mouth.

as the <u>Spirit</u> enabled them.

Two okay signs pull a string apart.

Holy Spirit!

When the day of Pentecost came,
they were all together in one place
Suddenly a sound like
the blowing of a violent wind
came from heaven
and filled the whole house
where they were sitting.
They saw what seemed
to be tongues of fire
that separated and came
to rest on each of them.
All of them
were filled with the Holy Spirit
and began to speak
in other tongues
as the Spirit enabled them.

Holy Spirit!
Acts 2:1-4

Winningham

Listen here!

Hoping for more of God's Word?

Find *Sing, Move, and Memorize!*
BOOKS
on **amazon.com**

Find *Sing, Move, and Memorize!*
VIDEO LESSONS
to help kids memorize God's word at **teacherspayteachers.com**

Made in the USA
Columbia, SC
10 February 2025